football's
new wave

Steve
McNair

Running & Gunning

By
MARK STEWART

THE MILLBROOK PRESS
BROOKFIELD, CONNECTICUT

M

THE MILLBROOK PRESS

Produced by
BITTERSWEET PUBLISHING
John Sammis, President
and
TEAM STEWART, INC.
RESEARCHED AND EDITED BY MIKE KENNEDY

Series Design and Electronic Page Makeup by
JAFFE ENTERPRISES
Ron Jaffe

All photos courtesy AP/ Wide World Photos, Inc. except the following:
Matthew Stockman/Allsport — Cover
Greg Jenson — Pages 6, 7, 8 (bottom right), 9, 13, 22 (bottom right), 33
Alcorn State University — 12, 14, 15, 16
The following images are from the collection of Team Stewart:
College Sports Publishing L.P. (©1995) — Page 20
Pinnacle Brands, Inc. (©1995) — Page 22 (top left)

Printed in the United States of America

Published by
The Millbrook Press, Inc.
2 Old New Milford Road
Brookfield, Connecticut 06804

www.millbrookpress.com

Library of Congress Cataloging-in-Publication Data

Stewart, Mark.
    Steve McNair: running & gunning / by Mark Stewart
    p.   cm.   — (Football's new wave)
    Includes index.
    ISBN 0-7613-1954-9 (lib. bdg.)
    1. McNair, Steve, 1973– —Juvenile literature. 2. Football players—United States—Biography—
Juvenile literature. [1. McNair, Steve, 1973 – . 2. Football players.] I. Title: Running & gunning. II.
Title. III. Series
GV939.M39 S84 2001
796.332'092--dc21
[B]   00-040205

1 3 5 7 9 10 8 6 4 2

Contents

Chapter	Page

A Family Thing

"I wanted my kids to have the same upbringing I had."
— LUCILLE McNAIR

There are two ways of looking at just about everything. You might say that this has been the story of Steve McNair's life. For instance, some would say that he grew up in desperation and poverty. But those who knew the McNairs would argue that Steve and his four brothers were raised in an atmosphere of cooperation, sharing, and love. In this case, there is more than a little truth in both.

Steve was the fourth of five sons born to Lucille and Selma McNair. They lived in a Mississippi farming town called Mount Olive. Their house was on Clarence Deen Road, which was named for the man who lived at the end of it. The McNairs' marriage ended when Steve was eight years old, leaving Lucille to raise five rambunctious boys on her own. She knew this would be a challenge, but she also believed there was a silver lining in this dark cloud.

Steve McNair has faced hard times and hard decisions throughout his life. When he looks back, it is still difficult for him to believe how far he has come.

Steve's little brother, Michael, is a running back. He plans to carry on the McNair family tradition and play for Mount Olive HS and Alcorn State.

One of 11 children herself, Steve's mother had been raised by *her* mother, "Grandma Hattie." The experience forced Lucille and her siblings to pull together, which in turn taught her the importance of a strong and loving family. When Selma left her in 1981, Lucille was determined to teach her children the same values. "She held us together when life was hard," says Steve.

Often life was very hard. The boys got up with the sun each morning so they could feed the chickens and pigs, pick vegetables, and get a jump on their other chores. Lucille worked the "graveyard" shift at a nearby electronics factory, starting after the boys were in bed and coming home as they finished their breakfast. She brought home less than $200 a week, which meant there was not much money for new clothes or toys or athletic equipment. The McNair boys knew they did not have the things other children had, but they never made much of a fuss. "We saw our mom struggle to support us," remembers Steve. "We saw it on her face when she came home. We also saw how she never complained or showed frustration."

Steve was the same way. In fact, through all of the ups and downs in his football life, people always have been amazed by his determination and his patience. People in Mount Olive were amazed by something else: Steve's skill at tree-climbing. All of the McNairs were athletic, but Steve was something special. He could scramble into the high branches in a matter of seconds—even faster when he messed up and knew his mother was coming after him. Lucille said Steve looked like a monkey going up a tree. That was all his brothers had to hear. From that day on, he was known as "Monk."

Steve's oldest brother, Fred, was the quarterback for Mount Olive High School. Naturally, Steve wanted to be a quarterback, too. He would attend every practice and watch his brother. Afterward, Fred and Steve would toss a ball around and talk about what it took to play the position. Steve began thinking it would be cool to play quarterback in the National Football League (NFL).

Steve used the lessons Fred taught him in pickup games on a field the neighborhood kids called "Mount Olive Arena." He had tremendous poise and judgment, even when being chased by a gang of tacklers. Steve knew he could outrun just about any kid in town, and if a receiver broke free, he knew he could hit him with a perfect spiral. In fact, the only player in Mount Olive who could give Steve a run for his money was Fred.

In time, this began to frustrate Steve. It seemed to him that all anyone could talk about was how good his brother was. One afternoon in ninth grade, Steve came home with tears streaming down his cheeks. He was sick and tired of hearing about Fred, he told his mother. He wanted to be better than Fred. He wanted to beat Fred. Lucille

Mount Olive is as quiet and laid-back today as it was when Steve was a kid.

"I owe my life to my mother. Without her I would cease to exist, so that's why I dedicate everything I do to her."
STEVE MCNAIR

calmed Steve down and told him it was all right to be competitive. However, this kind of competition was not good. Brothers had to stick together. Learn from Fred, she said, let him lead you. Do not make him the enemy. Steve understood. From that day to this one, her words have stayed with him. "Fred taught me absolutely everything I know," Steve says. "I can't thank him enough for giving me a road map—and then showing me how to take the short road when he's taken the longer one."

That map's starting point was Mount Olive High School, where Steve developed into a four-sport athlete and followed in Fred's footsteps as the starting quarterback for the Pirates. When Mount Olive was on defense, Steve became a defensive back. He was big, strong, fast, and smart. At any time he could make a game-breaking play. Steve used these same skills to become the star of the basketball team, where he "quarter-

backed" the varsity as a point guard. He also ran for the track team. Steve's fourth sport, baseball, might have been his best. The Seattle Mariners thought so. They offered him a contract to turn pro right after high school.

Steve was ready to take Seattle's offer. The family desperately needed the money. But both Lucille and Fred told him to turn it down. Steve still had his dream of becoming a famous quarter-back, and they encouraged him to pur-sue it. Steve declined the Mariners' contract. He believed that he had the

Steve's Air McNair Farm is easy to find—it is on Air McNair Road!

Steve leaves the competition behind as he scrambles for the winning score in the 1989 state championship game.

talent to make it to the NFL. So did many top colleges. They told Steve that if he came to play for them, he would be showcased to the NFL on national television. This sounded great at first, but Steve soon learned that these schools wanted him to be a safety, not a quarterback. They were less interested in his touchdown passes and spectacular runs than in his 30 interceptions, which tied the Mississippi high-school record.

Steve was not sure what to do. He had led Mount Olive to the state championship as a junior. As a senior, he had shattered all of Fred's school records, and earned All-America honors from *Super Prep* magazine. Why didn't anyone believe he could be a star quarterback in college?

Did You Know?

While Steve was in college, Fred played for teams in the Canadian Football League, NFL Europe, and Arena League Football. In 2000, Fred was a standout for the Florida Bobcats of the Arena League.

Moon over Mount Olive

When Steve was 11 years old, there was only one African-American quarterback in pro football, Warren Moon of the Houston Oilers. Moon was a great college player for the University of Washington. He could run and throw as well as anyone in the country. After he graduated, however, not a single NFL team wanted to give him a chance. They felt that he did not "fit the mold" of an NFL quarterback—and that his athletic talents and knowledge of the passing game might be best used as a defensive back. They did not believe Moon had what it took to be a "drop-back" quarterback in the pros. This was the fate of most black quarterbacks, and to some extent it still is. Moon decided to play quarterback in the Canadian Football League. In his first five seasons with the Edmonton Eskimos, he led the team to the Grey Cup (the CFL's "Super Bowl") each year. In 1984 the NFL finally opened its arms to Moon, and he signed with the Houston Oilers. Seven years later, he set the all-time record for pass completions in a season, with 404.

Young Leader

*"It was the family tradition.
I wanted to live up to
that name—McNair."*

— STEVE McNAIR

When Cardell Jones heard that schools like Florida State were recruiting Steve McNair, he gave up on the idea of carrying on a "family tradition." Jones, who was preparing for his first year as head of the Alcorn State football program, had seen Fred in college. He liked the idea of having Steve at the helm of the Braves' offense. But how could a tiny Division I-AA school tucked away in rural Mississippi compete with the football powerhouses talking to Steve? Little did Jones realize that the young man was leaning more and more toward following in his brother's footsteps once again.

Steve was tired of hearing scouts tell him why he could not be a quarterback. He and Jones began talking about Alcorn State. The more they talked, the more Steve felt it was the right place to be. His class at Mount Olive had just 42 kids in it. At a big

Steve and Fred were not the only McNairs to go to Alcorn State. Tim McNair also attended the school.

university, he feared he would be overwhelmed. Alcorn State was close to home (less than two hours away) and had just 3,300 students. And he knew from visiting Fred that the town of Lorman was a friendly place with a familiar flavor. In the end, the decision was easy. "It was just something in my heart," remembers Steve. "I wanted to go where I knew I could play quarterback."

Steve began the 1991 season as Alcorn State's second-string quarterback. Coach Jones had promised him he would get a chance to play, and he was true to his word. In the first quarter of the team's first game, Jones thought the offense looked sluggish. He turned to Steve and told him to get in the game. Steve was shocked. His teammates were shocked. The fans were shocked. They recognized the name, but knew little about him.

That changed quickly, as Steve tore Grambling's defense to shreds. He was a human highlight show. When the final gun sounded, Alcorn State was a 27–22 winner. All week long, no one on campus could talk about anything else but the miraculous McNair. Steve went on to have a marvelous freshman year, running and passing for a total of 3,199 yards—fourth best in all of Division I-AA football. The Braves finished 7–2–1, and went into 1992 as the top-ranked team in the Southwestern Athletic Conference (SWAC).

Steve was sensational again in 1992, throwing for 3,541 yards in 11 games. He completed 29 touchdown

Did You Know?

Fred's nickname in college was "Air McNair." Steve's was "Air II." The school put out a poster with a picture of Steve that said, "II Air is Divine."

passes and ran for 10 more scores, as the Braves fashioned a record of 7–4. Steve saved his best for the return match with Grambling. In the second quarter, he crumpled to

Steve's eyes light up
as he spots an open receiver.

the ground with a sprained ankle, and his teammates had to carry him off the field. But toughness was as much a part of Steve's game as his running and throwing. He retaped the ankle and got back on the field in the second half. Grambling had a fat lead, but Steve worked his magic and soon Alcorn State was within a few yards of the go-ahead score. With Steve limping badly, the Grambling defense decided to key on the Braves' running backs and receivers. Big mistake. Steve tucked the ball under his arm and pushed his broken body across the goal line with his last ounce of strength. On that play claims Coach Jones, he knew Steve was born to be a great quarterback.

When Steve decided to attend Alcorn State, he understood that he probably would be playing his entire college career in football's shadows. Alcorn State and the other schools in the SWAC offer an excellent education, but the pros consider them to have third-rate football programs. Although a few famous players—including Jerry Rice and Walter Payton—have come from this conference, no one ever hears much about its top teams and brightest stars.

Cardell Jones believes Steve was "born" to be a great quarterbck.

So imagine Steve's surprise when, during his junior year, he was the subject of feature articles in *Sports Illustrated* and *The Sporting News*. These publications reach millions of sports fans. Suddenly, Steve was a celebrity. What these magazines were saying about him was nothing new to his family, friends, and fans. He was big enough and tough enough for the pros, he could run faster than most running backs and receivers, and he could heave the ball 70 yards in the air. What bothered Steve's supporters was the suggestion that he might not be smart enough to be an NFL quarterback.

This was the same junk he had heard in high school from the college recruiters. Now that he had proved himself in college, he was facing the same prejudice from the pros. Was it, as many experts claimed, the fact that Steve was throwing against poor defenses? Or did it have something to do with the color of his skin? Here it was 1993, and there was just one other black starting quarterback (Rodney Peete) in the NFL besides Warren Moon. Steve did not care. He knew when his time came, he would simply give some team in the league no choice but to make him its quarterback.

Secretly, Steve was tickled to be mentioned as a pro prospect. In his mind, he was just one step closer to his dream. He was also closer to the big paycheck that would enable him to care for his family forever. The idea of leaving school after his junior year, however, did not sit well with him. Fred had had to leave Alcorn State before graduating, which meant Steve had a chance to be the first McNair to earn a college degree. He felt it would be like setting a record, or, more important, setting an example. "For generations to come, it will be just as normal to earn a college degree as it has been not to have one," Steve says.

Did You Know?

Steve's sensational junior season was marred by the death of his grandmother, Hattie. She had been like a second mother to the McNair brothers. He learned the news prior to the October game against Southern University, which Alcorn State lost 47–31.

Besides, Steve happened to love school. His football sometimes left little time for his classwork, but he stayed up late into the night to complete his assignments. He was a solid B student who participated in class, and he was a very good writer. Steve also knew that a football career ends when you are still young, so getting a diploma is very important. "No matter how much ability you have or how far you go, eventually your time in football is going to run out," he says. "I want a career after I retire."

Steve's junior season saw him turn in more terrific performances. Alcorn State's opponents came into games with defenses designed specifically to confuse Steve or rough him up. He responded with another 3,000-yard, 30-touchdown year and was named First-Team All-SWAC for the third-straight time. Steve was now on "the list" NFL teams keep of potential quarterbacks. To be seriously considered as a first-round pick, however, he would have to have an off-the-charts senior year.

"I didn't know I was that good!"
STEVE McNAIR

Run for the Record

chapter }

> *"I'll let my numbers speak for themselves."*
> — STEVE MCNAIR

The first game of Steve McNair's final college season ended in defeat for Alcorn State. But as losses go, it was not a terrible one. Grambling rolled up 62 points against Alcorn State, which forced Steve to try and score on every possession. He nearly did, throwing for 485 yards and five touchdowns to make the score 62–56. On the game's final play, he lofted a perfect pass into receiver Percy Singleton's arms as he galloped toward the end zone. Once again, it looked like Steve had pulled one out against Grambling. But this time Grambling got a break. Singleton dropped the ball, and Alcorn State lost.

Steve "morphs" into the Heisman Trophy on the cover of the Braves' 1994 media guide.

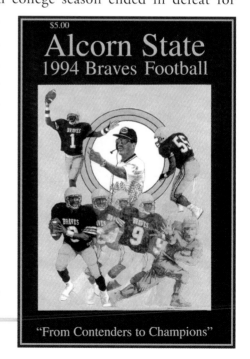

$5.00

Alcorn State
1994 Braves Football

"From Contenders to Champions"

Did You Know?

After Steve's marvelous 1994 comeback against Grambling fell short, coach Eddie Robinson rushed over to console him. "You're the best," college football's all-time winningest coach told Steve.

Chattanooga, Steve made headlines again. This time he ran and passed for a combined 647 yards—the most ever in a Division I-AA game! He also threw eight touchdown passes. Suddenly, his doubters from previous years were ready to hand him the Heisman Trophy, college football's MVP award. Steve took all the attention in stride. He knew the chances of a player from a little school like Alcorn State winning the Heisman were zero. He would have to break every record in the book before they considered him.

Or maybe just one record. No college quarterback had ever averaged 4,000 yards in total offense over a four-year career. The closest had been Ty Detmer, who ran and passed for 15,049 while at Brigham Young University. Steve wanted that record. It might not prove he was the best player in the country, or guarantee him a job in the NFL, but it would certainly be a nice way to crown a regal college career.

Steve was a man on a mission in 1994. He gobbled up yards at an amazing rate, passing for nearly 5,000 and running for almost 1,000 more. Steve broke Detmer's record—and broke his own single-game mark—with 649 yards against Southern University. Despite

Ty Detmer, whose career yardage record Steve eclipsed in 1994.

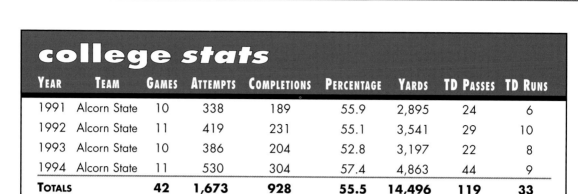

college *stats*

Year	Team	Games	Attempts	Completions	Percentage	Yards	TD Passes	TD Runs
1991	Alcorn State	10	338	189	55.9	2,895	24	6
1992	Alcorn State	11	419	231	55.1	3,541	29	10
1993	Alcorn State	10	386	204	52.8	3,197	22	8
1994	Alcorn State	11	530	304	57.4	4,863	44	9
Totals		**42**	**1,673**	**928**	**55.5**	**14,496**	**119**	**33**

college *achievements*

All-American 1994
Walter Peyton Award 1994
Heisman Trophy Finalist 1994
All SWAC 1991–1994
NCAA Career Total Yardage Leader

being hobbled by a sore hamstring, he finished the year in style by completing a record 52 passes against Youngstown State in the I-AA playoffs.

Although he had broken more than a dozen records as a college quarterback, Steve would face his biggest challenges in the months ahead. Pro scouts would be

watching his every move, first at the college All-Star games and then at the NFL scouting combines. Finally, Steve would have a chance to go head-to-head with the top talent in the country.

Although throwing on the run was Steve's specialty, he could stay in the pocket and deliver the long bomb as well as anyone.

Proof Positive

chapter **4**

> *"Pressure is what you make of it. It makes me play harder."*
> — **STEVE McNAIR**

As the NFL Draft neared, Steve began popping up on a lot of magazine covers.

The Senior Bowl was Steve McNair's first stop on the way to the NFL. At Alcorn State, his strategy had been to take the snap, sprint toward the sideline, and force the defense into blowing its pass coverage. If Steve did not spot a receiver, he would spy an opening, pick up a blocker or two, and carry the ball himself—often for a huge gain. In the NFL, quarterbacks are expected to play a different game. A team that has

Steve is congratulated after being announced as the number-one draft choice of the Houston Oilers.

invested millions in a passer does not want to see him running unless it is a last resort. Also, designing effective pass patterns and blocking schemes is hard to do if the quarterback does not stay in one place.

Steve knew the NFL scouts at the Senior Bowl questioned whether he could be a "drop-back" or "pocket" passer. So during practices and in the game itself, he showed the pros he could play their kind of football. "My plan was to sit in the pocket and wait for things to develop," Steve says. "I didn't want to take things all on myself."

The scouts came back from the Senior Bowl raving. McNair, they said, looked like the real deal. The next test came at the combines, where the top 300 or so pro prospects are put through their paces while the entire NFL evaluates them. Part of this tryout involves mental testing. Steve passed with flying colors—the results revealed a patient, thoughtful, and intelligent young man who was perfectly suited to be a professional quarterback. So much for not being "smart" enough!

The team most impressed by Steve was the Houston Oilers. They held the third pick in the spring draft, and they needed a quarterback. Warren Moon had led the Oilers to the American Football Conference (AFC) Central Division title in 1993 but was traded the following season to the Minnesota Vikings. While Moon led the Vikings to the top of their division in 1994, the Oilers collapsed. The team won just two games, and coach Jack Pardee was replaced by Jeff Fisher with six games to go. The once-proud franchise was in shambles.

The Oilers selected Steve with their pick and quickly signed him to a seven-year contract. Coach Fisher warned Steve that there would be pressure to play him right away, but that he would not become the starter until the team felt he was ready. Steve understood. It was for his benefit as well as Fisher's. Steve would watch and learn, behind starter Chris Chandler and backup Will Furrer. He would also work with quarterback "guru" Jerry Rhome, whom the Oilers hired specifically to work with Steve.

During training camp, Steve tried to absorb as much about the pro game as he could. This meant participating in

Did You Know?

Jerry Rhome's most famous pupil prior to Steve was superstar Troy Aikman.

It took Steve two years to make Houston's starting lineup. Smart collectors bought up his football cards while he was still sitting on the bench.

drills, watching hours of game film, and studying the team playbook until he knew it backward and forward. Steve was amazed at how much larger, and faster, and more precise the pro game was—and this was a last-place team he had joined!

The Oilers held their own in 1995, winning seven games and losing nine. The defense did its job, Chandler had a fine year, and Steve learned a lot. He got into a couple of late-season games, against the Lions and the Jets, and looked good. In 1996, Steve was still the backup, but he played more and more as the year progressed. In the season's 13th game, he started against the Jacksonville Jaguars and threw for more than 300 yards. The more Coach Fisher saw of Steve, the more he liked him. He had developed a sense of when to play it safe and when to take risks. He was not panicking in tight spots. And he had learned not to force passes that had a low percentage of success. These things told Fisher that Steve was ready to be his starter in 1997.

Did You Know?

After Steve signed a $28 million dollar contract with the Oilers in 1995, he bought his mother a little surprise: a beautiful new house just outside Mount Olive. When Lucille saw it she broke down crying. The house was located on the same land on which she had picked cotton as a girl.

Stepping Into the Spotlight

chapter

> *"My goal? To win a couple of Super Bowls!"*
> — STEVE McNAIR

The decision to make Steve McNair the Oilers' number-one quarterback in 1997 was a popular one with everyone except Chris Chandler. For two years, Chandler had complained loudly that the team was spending too much time getting Steve ready to take his job, and not enough helping him keep it. Chandler, in fact, barely spoke to Steve. In games when Chandler was sick or injured and Steve took his place, he offered the young quarterback little advice.

Steve kept his chin up and refused to let Chandler's childish behavior affect him. Besides, getting the "cold shoulder" was nothing compared to the frustration of not playing. Looking back on the experience, however, Steve sees that waiting his turn made him a stronger player. "Sitting out those two years made it so nothing I could see on the field would ever surprise me."

Steve and Mechelle Cartwright were married in June 1997. More than 1,500 friends and family members attended the wedding.

The other players knew how tough it was to be ignored by a veteran, and they respected how Steve responded. He looked like the kind of leader a team would happily follow. Chandler was traded to the Falcons before the 1997 season, ending the quarterback controversy. Also shown the door was Jerry Rhome, who had allied himself with Chandler.

The Oilers, now located in Tennessee, were finally Steve's team.

What the new fans in Tennessee did not fully understand was that the Oilers were still taking shape as a team. Eddie George, the second-year sensation from Ohio State, was a big, bruising runner who wore down defenses. The Oilers' young and enthusiastic defense wore down opposing offenses. Steve's job was to keep the score close, then deliver the knockout blow in the fourth quarter. This did not make for very interesting football. Fans wanted Steve to run and throw long bombs, as he had in his college days. But Steve knew that what might be good for his stats would not help the team win. "It's always team first," he maintains. "It's not ever one person who does it all."

Although inconsistent in his first year as a starter, Steve did manage to provide his share of thrills, and the team finished with a respectable 8–8 record. Steve also did something very unusual for a quarterback: He led the NFL in yards per carry as a runner, edging Barry Sanders 6.7 to 6.1. Steve carried the ball 101 times (mostly when he could not find an open receiver) and gained 674 yards.

In 1998 the Oilers took important steps toward becoming an AFC powerhouse. Steve had an excellent year, completing 289 passes for 3,228 yards. This forced defenders to play back more, which in turn gave Steve more room when he decided to run. He carried the ball 77 times for 559 yards, averaging 7.3 per try. Against the four other teams in its division, the Oilers went 7–1. This was a sign that they were ready to take control of the AFC West. But against everyone else, the team went 1–7. Close losses to three bad teams (the Bears, Chargers, and Seahawks) ruined Tennessee's season. Once again the team's record was 8–8.

Despite another so-so year, two very good things happened in 1998. The team started construction on a new stadium, and the fans got to vote for a new name. For Steve's first two years in Tennessee, the team played in college stadiums. In 1997 they occupied the Liberty Bowl in Memphis.

Steve takes the field for his team's first game in Tennessee.

At 6'2", 225 pounds, Steve is big enough to hold his own in the pocket. That makes him a prime target for pass rushers. Notice the extra protective padding under his uniform.

In 1998 they played in Vanderbilt Stadium in Nashville. Attendance was poor, the fields were in bad shape because of the college games, and the players had to clear their stuff out of the locker rooms after each game. Even though the fans who did show up rooted them on, the Oilers always felt like they were playing on the road.

Also, no one understood why the team was still called the Oilers. An "Oiler" is someone who works in the oil fields, which made sense in Houston, where oil is the biggest industry. The state of Tennessee produces some oil, but certainly not enough to call its only pro football team the Oilers. In 1998 the team held a contest to find a new name for the following year. Of the thousands of names submitted, the winner was "Titans." Steve and his teammates also got snappy new uniforms. They were happy to shed the powder-blue jerseys left over from their Houston days.

Did You Know?

A Titan is a huge, mythical being. It is also a popular sports name. In fact, during the early 1960s, New York's American Football League team was called the Titans for several years before becoming the Jets.

Turning the Corner

chapter **6**

> "We feel we're better than 8-8 ... we just have to get over that hump. Good things are going to happen once we get over that barrier."
>
> — STEVE McNair

In many ways, the worst thing you can be in football is a .500 team. If you lose exactly as many games as you win—as the Titans had for three years in a row—it is hard to tell whether you are getting better or getting worse. In Tennessee's case, Steve seemed to be improving, but Eddie George looked exhausted at the end of the 1998 season. Had three years of constant pounding begun to take its toll on the young star? The team had developed a good short-passing attack, but it lacked big-time receivers. Frank Wycheck was small for a tight end, Kevin Dyson was young and inexperienced, and Yancey Thigpen was coming off a leg injury. Would Steve have the talent he needed to improve the Titan attack? The defense specialized in bone-crunching tackles but had a terrible pass rush. Does it matter how hard you hit some-

"Steve does what we ask him to do. He can run 62 yards and score. He can throw 62 yards and score."
JEFF FISHER

one if he has already caught a 15-yard pass against you? These were the questions the Titans faced heading into the 1999 season.

Jeff Fischer felt his offense was in fine shape. He had a couple of good tackles named Jon Runyan and Brad Hopkins, and they seemed ready to turn in superstar seasons. If they could handle opposing pass rushers, then the Titans could send their tight ends and running backs out on pass plays, and Steve would have his choice of four or five receivers.

The defense was another story. Coach Fisher needed to find a great pass rusher. Then everything else would fall into place. To his delight, Jevon Kearse of the University of Florida was still available when the Titans picked 16th in the 1999 draft. Kearse was large and fast and mean. His nickname was "The Freak," because no one had ever seen such a big man move so much like a little man. For him, every play was a seek-and-destroy mission. Fisher put him on the defensive line and told him to wipe out whoever had the ball.

By Week One of the 1999 season, all of the pieces seemed to be in place. The blockers were blocking, the tacklers were tackling, the runners were running, and the receivers were receiving. Steve? He was looking cool and confident. There was a sense

Tennessee's defense came together in 1999 when the ferocious Jevon Kearse joined the team.

The Tennessee Titans got more than a new name in 1999.
They got a new home—Adelphia Coliseum in Nashville.

in the Titans' camp that this was going to be a special year. They were not going to blow anyone out, but they were not going to give away any games either.

The Titans also planned to "unfold" Steve's game a little more. They would stick with short, safe passes, but every so often they wanted him to "stretch" the defense by trying for a big play. All summer, they practiced this in special long-ball drills. In the season's opening game, against the Bengals, Steve showed he could throw deep when he hit Thigpen with a 47-yard touchdown pass. In all he completed 21 of 32 passes for 341 yards and three touchdowns.

Did You Know?

In 1995, Neil O'Donnell (see page 31) and Yancey Thigpen were teammates on the AFC champion Pittsburgh Steelers. They connected for a team-record 85 catches that season.

All of the questions surrounding the Titans during the off-season seemed to be answered in one game. Fisher could not have been happier...until he saw Steve in the locker room. His back was giving him excruciating pain. He had an inflamed disk, and needed an immediate operation. Luckily, the team had a capable backup named Neil O'Donnell. O'Donnell had led the Pittsburgh Steelers to the Super Bowl four years earlier. During the five games Steve missed, O'Donnell guided the Titans to a 4–1 record.

He played so well that some thought Steve should stay on the bench. But not the players. They knew Steve was the man.

Steve and Neil O'Donnell compare notes during his first day back after back surgery.

Steve's first game back found the Titans playing the surprise team of the year, the St. Louis Rams. They were led by a previously unknown quarterback named Kurt Warner, who was having a fabulous season. Kearse, who was blossoming in his role as a one-man sack machine, hounded Warner all game. Steve, whose job was to get a lead and eat up the clock, did just that. In the first quarter he threw a pair of touchdown passes and ran the ball in for a third score to give his team a 21–0 lead. The rest of the game was a war. The Rams clawed back and managed

to set up the game-tying field goal. But St. Louis missed the kick, and Tennessee escaped with a victory.

It took Steve more than a month to get completely healthy and regain his timing. Fortunately, he played well enough to win four of the six games the team played during that span. Then the Titans won their final four games—including a 41–14 thrashing of the division-leading Jacksonville Jaguars—and made the playoffs with a 13–3 record.

Steve had led the Titans to a Wild Card berth despite a bad case of "turf toe." It is one of the most painful injuries in sports. Every step sends a shock wave of pain through the body. It makes playing football extremely unpleasant. Most players who get it simply sit out until it feels better, but this was not an option for Steve. The team had not made the playoffs once since he was drafted, and he was not going to miss this opportunity. Quarterbacks are in pain all the time, he reasoned, so how bad could a little more be?

Steve barrels ahead against the Rams during a 24–21 victory. They would meet again before the season was over.

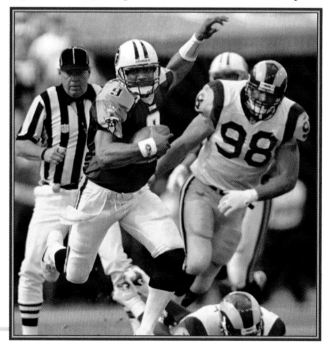

My Mama Said . . .

Want to know about Steve? Just ask his mom, Lucille!

"Steve is like me. He does not show his emotions very easily."

"Steve has gone from the bottom to the top. He knows how to work for what he wants, and how to earn it."

"It means a lot to Steve to show people what he can accomplish."

"During college he was a young man. Now he considers himself a man, a father, a leader. He wants to be a role model."

"The black quarterback thing, the way people think about him as a quarterback, he is going to convince people they have to rethink their position."

Comeback Kids

chapter 7

*"He's got what
I call personality
under pressure."*

— LES STECKEL, TITANS'
OFFENSIVE COORDINATOR

To be a winner in the NFL, you need to be tough and you need to be talented. Sometimes you need to be lucky, too. Steve McNair's toughness was unquestioned, and obviously he had a world of talent. But considering the injuries and pain Steve had had to battle, 1999 was not what you would call a lucky year. That would change against the Buffalo Bills in the Wild Card game.

*"If you were going to put together a list of all
the things you can't coach—poise, ability to lead,
competitiveness, responsibility—he has them all."*

JEFF FISHER

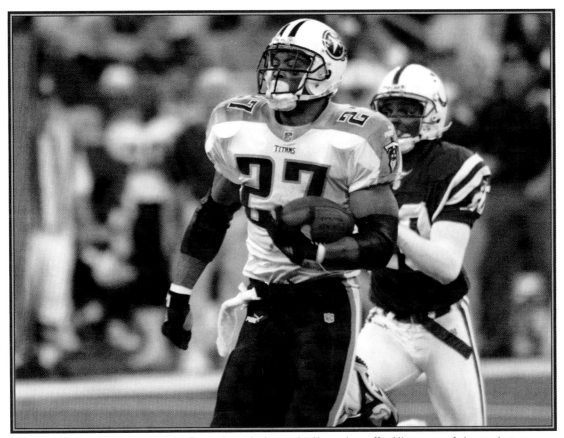

Eddie George sprints for a touchdown in the playoffs. His powerful running gives the Titans one of the most balanced attacks in all of football.

The Bills did an excellent job of keeping Steve and Eddie George under control. The Titans did just as well against Buffalo. Every yard in this game was a hard one; every point was precious. The first score came on a safety, as the Titan defense tackled Buffalo quarterback Rob Johnson in his own end zone. A few minutes later, Steve carried the ball around right end and scored to put Tennessee up 9–0. An Al Del Greco field goal made it 12–0 at the half.

The third quarter saw the Bills come roaring back. They scored the first time they got the ball and then made another touchdown to take a 13–12 lead. Late in the fourth quarter, the Titans began moving the ball again. On a crucial third-down play, Steve made a super run to keep the drive alive. Then Del Greco booted another field goal to make the score 15–13 Tennessee. All the Titans had to do was hold the Bills for a

No Buffalo tacklers are in sight as Kevin Dyson finishes his remarkable run. The wild play saved the Titans' season.

couple of minutes. But Johnson caught fire and guided his team into field-goal range. With just a few seconds left, Doug Christie split the uprights with a field goal to put Buffalo back on top 16–15. Steve watched helplessly from the sideline as the Bills stole the game away. All that remained was Buffalo's kickoff and the final gun. Then the season would be over.

Christie and the Bills lined up for the kick. He booted the ball short, trying to keep it away from Tennessee's fastest players. The ball ended up in the hands of Frank Wycheck, the tight end. Wycheck was Steve's most reliable receiver, but he was a slow, lumbering man. He had no chance to score. As the Buffalo players closed in, Wycheck began to move toward the right sideline. Then, suddenly, he spun around and heaved a long lateral across the field to Kevin Dyson, one of the swiftest runners on the team. Dyson caught the ball and looked ahead of him. To his amazement, there was no one between himself and the goal line. The Buffalo player whose job it was to guard that side of the field had run toward Wycheck with everyone else. When he saw the ball go to Dyson and realized his mistake, he was unable to get back in time. Dyson sprinted into the end zone untouched. Unbelievably, incredibly, the Titans had won!

After such an unexpected victory, teams often suffer a letdown. Coach Fisher was not about to let this happen. He made sure his players understood who their next opponent was—and what it would take to beat them. The Indianapolis Colts had come into their own in 1999. Peyton Manning was the best young quarterback in the NFL, and running back Edgerrin James had gained more than 1,000 yards in a remarkable rookie season. Receiver Marvin Harrison had great moves, a sprinter's speed, and a quarterback who could get the ball to him. In other words, the only way to keep the Colts from scoring a lot of points was to keep their offense off the field. This became Steve's job. The more time the Tennessee offense could control the football, the less time Manning and his crew would have with it. In a sense, Steve was the Titans' key "defensive" player in this game.

The plan worked to perfection. Steve handed the ball to George and let him punch holes in the Indianapolis defense. Then he would throw safe, short passes. Twice in the first half, this strategy got the Titans into field-goal range.

Steve's running ability made a difference in every game he played in 1999. During the playoffs, he was a lethal weapon.

And twice Del Greco's kicks were true. Meanwhile, Manning struggled against Tennessee's swarming defense. Coach Fisher, an old defensive back, had designed new coverage schemes to confuse the young quarterback, and they worked. Although the Colts were able to move the football, they could not come up with the big play when they needed it. At halftime, Indianapolis was ahead by only three points, 9–6.

During the intermission, Steve and his teammates agreed that one major play would probably decide the game. The only question was which team would pull it off? The answer came just 90 seconds into the third quarter. With the ball on his own 32 yard line, Steve handed off to George. The Titans' "go-to" guy spotted an opening and burst

Peyton Manning congratulates Steve for his comeback win against the Colts.

through it. Then he made a beautiful cut to reach the open field. From there it was a footrace to the end zone, which George won.

The score was now 13–9. Steve chewed up the clock for the rest of the second half and put six more points on the board. Manning managed to lead his team to a late touchdown, but by then the game was under Tennessee's control. Once again, Steve and the Titans had defied the odds. And now they were headed to the AFC Championship Game.

Tennessee's foe in the title game was the Jacksonville Jaguars, a team they had already played twice in 1999. These opponents knew each other very well. In the second meeting Steve had burned the Jags with five touchdown passes. Coach Fisher decided to change his normal game plan and let Steve try to repeat his magical performance. It was a big risk. If Steve could not put points on the board, Jacksonville's quarterback, Mark Brunell, surely would.

In the first half, Tennessee's swarming defense kept Brunell under control. But the Jaguar pass defense did an excellent job, too. After 30 minutes, the score was 14–10 in favor of Jacksonville. In the locker room at halftime, some of the Titans were muttering to themselves. The game plan wasn't working—why didn't they stick with what had gotten them there?

When the players looked to see how Steve was acting, they saw a poised and confident leader. Steve knew that the second half would be different. Although both defenses were playing well, there was a big difference: Brunell was getting creamed by the Tennessee pass rush. But the Jaguars were not laying a hand on Steve. They were huffing and puffing all over the field, unable to catch him. He knew this would take its toll in the second half.

On the Titans' very first possession, Steve led the team to the go-ahead score. And sure enough, as the final 30 minutes ticked away the poor Jaguars could barely catch their breath. They never scored another point, and could only watch as Steve ran them ragged in a 33–14 victory. For the first time in franchise history, the team was headed to the Super Bowl.

Steve acknowledges the fans at Adelphia Coliseum
after the Titans returned from Jacksonville as AFC champions.

Quest for the Crown

chapter **8**

"When I get on the field, I feel unstoppable."
— STEVE MCNAIR

All Steve McNair had done during the playoffs was win. What more could a quarterback be asked to do? Yet according to the press covering Super Bowl XXXIV, he should have had better statistics! Steve's opponent in the big game, Kurt Warner of the St. Louis Rams, had thrown for more than 4,000 yards and 40 touchdowns in 1999. Steve, on the other hand, had just one 300-yard game all year. And in the AFC Championship he had only thrown for 112 yards.

What could Steve say? In the very same contest, he had been the Titans' top rusher, and he had scored two touchdowns by himself. But for some reason, none of this seemed to count. To this day he does not understand why he and the Titans were such underdogs going into the Super Bowl. "I'm out there to play football," Steve says. "Regardless of what numbers I put up, people talk about not throwing touchdowns, or not getting 300 yards passing. We're winning! That's what counts! You have to do what it takes to win."

The Rams knew that Steve was a lot scarier than his numbers. They knew they would have their hands full. St. Louis's one major weakness was that it could not always stop a good running attack. Eddie George and Steve McNair would most definitely put the Rams to the test.

As Super Bowl XXXIV began, it looked as if Steve would have to throw for 300 yards and a bunch of touchdowns. The Rams' defense was having good luck against George, while their offense was murdering the Titans. Time after time, Warner was able to move the ball deep into Tennessee territory. Fortunately, the defense held when it had to and the Rams managed just three field goals. Steve got the Titans into field-goal range once in the first half, but Al Del Greco's kick

Steve tries to establish Tennessee's ground game against the Rams in the first quarter of Super Bowl XXXIV.

was blocked. At halftime the Rams were up, but only by a score of 9–0.

This time there was much optimism in the Tennessee locker room. The players had been in this position in each of their last two games and won. Steve looked confident, the defense was doing well, and the Titans knew they could easily erase a halftime deficit.

Even Steve had to worry a little, however, when the Rams made the first touchdown of the second half. Now behind 16–0, Steve went to work. His short passes found their

Steve and Jeff Fisher discuss strategy as the clock winds down on Super Bowl XXXIV.

mark; his mad scrambles wore out the St. Louis linemen. And Eddie George began hammering away at the defense. With 14 seconds left in the third quarter, he plowed into the end zone to make the score 16–7.

Tennessee's first possession in the fourth quarter also resulted in a touchdown, as Steve put together another long drive and George scored again to cut the deficit to 16–13. With just over two minutes to go in the game, Steve got the ball close enough for another field-goal try. Del Greco made the kick, and the score was knotted 16–16.

The Titans kicked off, and the Rams prepared for what everyone thought would be the game's final drive. Warner had two minutes to score or the game would go into overtime. On the first play, however, he completed a pass to speedy Isaac Bruce, who took it all the way for a backbreaking 73-yard touchdown. Steve could hardly believe it. Just as in the Buffalo game, a late score had put the Titans in a deep, deep hole.

Only now, Steve actually had time to climb out of it. The Rams had scored so quickly that there was still more than a minute left. Steve went into "the zone," doing everything in the book to give his team a scoring chance. On one unforgettable play,

Steve took the snap with just 22 seconds on the clock. He rolled right, searching desperately for a receiver. A pair of St. Louis pass rushers converged on him, but he somehow managed to shed them. Then he fired a perfect strike to Kevin Dyson on the 10-yard line and called timeout with just a few ticks left.

On the sideline, Steve discussed his options with the coaching staff. The Titans had time for one final play. If they scored, they would have a chance to tie or even win the game. Steve knew the Rams were expecting him to throw to his big tight end, Frank Wycheck. Finally, the

> ## Did You Know?
> Steve's 64 rushing yards set a Super Bowl record for quarterbacks.

decision was made to send Wycheck across the middle as a decoy and have Dyson "sneak in" behind him. If Wycheck drew double-coverage, Dyson would be open for a short pass and an easy touchdown. If Steve could not find a receiver, he could always try to run it in himself.

Steve barked out the signals, surveyed the defense, took the ball from the center, and quickly dropped back. He watched Wycheck rumble across the middle and saw that he was indeed drawing an extra man—linebacker Robert Jones. Just as the Titans had hoped, Dyson broke free and darted toward the middle as Steve cocked his arm to throw.

Jones suddenly realized what was going on and veered back toward Dyson. He was too late to stop Steve's pass, which was perfect. Jones made a desperate lunge and man-

pro stats

Year	Team	Games	Attempts	Completions	%	Yards	TD Passes	TD Runs
1995	Houston Oilers	4	80	41	51.2	569	3	0
1996	Houston Oilers	9	143	88	61.5	1,197	6	2
1997	Tennessee Oilers	16	415	216	52.0	2,665	14	8
1998	Tennessee Oilers	16	492	289	58.7	3,228	15	4
1999	Tennessee Titans	11	331	187	56.5	2,179	12	8
Totals		**56**	**1,461**	**821**	**56.2**	**9,838**	**50**	**22**

pro achievements

NFL Yards-Per-Carry Leader 1997
AFC Champion 1999

Kevin Dyson strains to reach the end zone, as Robert Jones of the Rams brings him down. This was the final play in the most thrilling Super Bowl ever played.

aged to wrap his arms around Dyson's legs as he sprinted toward the goal line. Dyson began to fall. He stretched his arm out in an attempt to get the ball over the goal line. Steve's heart stopped as, for a split second, it looked liked Dyson might perform his second miracle of the postseason. But when the whistle blew and there was no touchdown call, he knew the Titans had come up just a yard short. "It was a one-on-one play," Steve says, "and they made the play. I thought we were going to get it in."

The final score read St. Louis 23, Tennessee 16. It was a shame anyone had to lose. Thanks to Steve and his teammates—and, of course, the Rams—football fans had been treated to the most exciting Super Bowl in history. There would be no more questions about Steve's ability to lead a team, to move an offense, or to put points on the scoreboard. He had done all of these things under the toughest conditions imaginable.

Steve and Mechelle wave to the fans in Nashville. The city threw a parade for the Titans two days after the Super Bowl.

Level Head, Lion's Heart

chapter 9

"I'm a country guy from Mississippi who keeps it simple."

— STEVE MCNAIR

When you come as close to winning it all as Steve McNair did in Super Bowl XXXIV, the fans expect nothing less than total victory after that. Is that too much to ask? Will it force Steve to try to "do it all," as he did back in college? Not a chance—he guarantees it. "The object of the game is to move the chains," Steve says. "My slogan is still 'Don't force the ball.' Besides, I've never believed anyone could put more pressure on me than I put on myself. People expect great things from me. I expect great things from myself."

What the experts expect from Steve is more of the maturity and leadership

Did You Know?

If Tyler McNair (born in 1998) becomes a quarterback, that will make three generations of quarterbacks in Steve's family. "We had a long chain of family members that were quarterbacks," he says. "From my uncle to my cousins to my brothers."

he showed on the way to the Super Bowl. They point to the late-season game against

Steve can finally relax. By leading his team to the Super Bowl, he has answered those who questioned his ability to be a winning quarterback in the NFL.

the Jaguars as a turning point in his career. In that 44–14 victory, Steve stepped up and took charge as he never had before. More important, that was the day every last player on the Titans became convinced that Steve could lead them to the Super Bowl. The next step is for Steve to trust his teammates as much as they trust him. When that happens, no one doubts that the Titans will become a very special team.

Of course, there is no longer any doubt about Steve McNair. He is a very special player, and a very special person. No matter what stands in his path, he always finds the smartest way around or over it. And on those rare occasions when Steve cannot get around or over an obstacle, *look out*—he is more than happy to put his head down and run right through it!

Index